PRESTO!
LEARN HYPNO!

DR. JOHN H EDGETTE

No fluff! This book tells you exactly what you need to do to hypnotize somebody. I was intrigued by the three-sentence induction, which I think is going to be taught as a core strategy for decades to come. In this book, you will discover more about hypnosis than most books that are ten times its size. I am amazed that Dr. John Edgette was able to cut to the essence of creating hypnotic benefit as easily as he did and with depth. If you are new to hypnosis, do yourself a favor and use this book as your starting point. If you have lots of experience as a hypnotist, do yourself a favor and get this book so that you can return to the simplicity of highly effective hypnosis.

— DR. RICHARD NONGARD,
AUTHOR OF THE SELF-HYPNOSIS
SOLUTION AND THE SEVEN MOST
EFFECTIVE METHODS OF SELF-
HYPNOSIS

Dr. John Edgette has written an amazing book! So much content in just a few pages! Dr. Edgette is a master of the technology of hypnotic inductions, creating hypnotic suggestions and bringing out hypnotic phenomena for interventions.

I have been privileged to observe Dr. Edgette use hypnotism in his psychotherapy practice and to benefit from his previous books! His style of writing has translated technical instructions so gracefully that the beginner and the experienced practitioner can both benefit from this type of instruction! Great quick read, but it unlocks the field of hypnotism in a way that allows the average person to begin hypnotizing!! I highly recommend both Dr. John Edgette and his NEW BOOK. A small book, heavy with powerful techniques! I will continue to use Dr. Edgette's larger textbook, The Handbook of Hypnotic Phenomena in Psychotherapy in my advanced classes, but I will recommend this smaller book for all of my students!

— WILLIAM MITCHELL M.DIV., BCH, CI, ORGANIZER OF THE HEARTLAND HYPNOSIS CONFERENCE ST. LOUIS, MO; LEAD HYPNOTHERAPIST FOR PERSONAL MOTIVATION HYPNOSIS CLINICS SPRINGFIELD AND DECATUR, IL

Copyright © 2022 by Dr. John H. Edgette
All rights reserved.
Published by John Galt & Associates
ISBN: 978-1-7354802-9-9

Portions of this book have appeared in prior books by the author. That material has been expanded, edited, and updated for this book.

All rights reserved. No part of this publication may be reproduced, distributed, or transmitted in any form or by any means, including photocopying, recording, or other electronic or mechanical methods, without the prior written permission from the author, except in the case of brief quotations embodied in critical reviews and certain other non-commercial uses permitted by copyright law.

This publication is not meant to provide medical or psychological advice. It is for educational or informational purposes only. Case examples are entirely fictional and any resemblance to an actual person is entirely coincidental.

Due to the hypnotic elements in this book it is inadvisable to listen to it while driving, flying a plane, or operating heavy machinery.

First Printing: October 2021

Dr. John H. Edgette
P.O. Box 1271
Fairfield, Iowa
USA
1 917-806-1850
john@edgettetherapy.com

To Milton H Erickson MD, another mentor in absentia.

CONTENTS

1. Introduction to Induction — 1
2. Preparation of the Subject for Hypnosis — 3
3. Induction Method #1: Double Binds — 7
4. Induction Method #2: Conscious – Unconscious Dissociative Statements — 9
5. Hypnotic Induction Method #3: ABC and 1, 2, 3 — 11
6. Induction Method #4: The Three-Sentence Induction — 15
7. Induction Method #5: Regression to a Past Highly Relaxed State — 19
8. Ratification and Deepening — 23
9. The Art of Giving Suggestions - To Self and Others — 29
10. What are Hypnotic Phenomena? — 35
11. Doing It: Hypnotic Phenomena — 43
12. De-hypnotizing Your Client — 53
13. Ending This Trance — 57
14. List of Hypnotic Steps — 59

About Dr. John H. Edgette — 61
Also by Dr. John H Edgette — 63

1

INTRODUCTION TO INDUCTION

You are about to read the shortest book ever written to teach hypnosis. Yet, it covers every essential part of the hypnotic experience. Reading this book won't make you an expert, nor will it even make you a journeyman. WHAT IT WILL DO IS MAKE YOU A FULLY COMPETENT BEGINNER, ABLE TO COMPLETELY HYPNOTIZE MOST PEOPLE.

By reading this book, you will learn all the stages and steps of hypnosis! Start to finish, soup to nuts, beginning to end, alpha to omega.

You will learn:

- how to prepare your subject for hypnosis
- how to get started using one of 5 induction strategies.
- how to deepen the trance
- how to activate the subjects unconscious mind to receive suggestions

- how to formulate and give suggestions for change
- how to elicit hypnotic phenomena for transformation.
- how to end the hypnotic experience

Once you learn it, you will start doing it! It is best to pick mentally healthy and stable individuals so it will be easier for you as a beginner.

You will develop your skills by reading and taking online courses. In those courses you can develop a support group of peers. You will also meet teachers whom you can get supervised by, for a fee of course, and practice, practice, practice!

Before you know it you will feel comfortable doing stage shows and helping people change their bad habits!! So read on!

2

PREPARATION OF THE SUBJECT FOR HYPNOSIS

First off, as a reminder, the chapters that follow are designed for those who are learning hypnosis for the first time or those who once learned and need a refresher. If you fall into the first category, it would be a good idea to supplement what you find here with additional reading, zoom teaching, and some one-on-one consulting with a very experienced practitioner. In the meantime, readers are most welcome to e-mail me with any questions.

Hypnotizing someone is incredibly easy. Hypnotizing someone else so that they can hypnotize themselves is easier still, and the easiest of all is to hypnotize yourself. Whether you are in this to entrance your client, help your client entrance themselves, or put yourself under, the procedures in the following chapters, taken as a whole, accomplish that mission.

Hypnosis has often been made to seem very hard, technical, mysterious, and requiring incredible precision. There are probably at least three reasons for this. One reason is that students are held in constant awe and confusion and continue to pay high prices for multitudes of courses. The second reason may be that the teachers wish to see themselves as very advanced, educated, scientific, wise, and desire to have their students see them in the same way. A third reason may be that there is then a greater placebo effect from the use of hypnosis as a procedure.

Yet simple it remains.

To start, find out from your subject what they have heard or experienced about hypnosis. Affirm the validity of all reports describing how hypnosis was a very helpful tool in enlisting the aid of the subconscious mind in overcoming a problem such as an addiction or pain. If the client cites anything that they worry about in connection with hypnosis, assure them with confidence that this is an unneeded worry. ***There is absolutely no loss of control in hypnosis. People cannot be made to do anything that they do not want to do while in trance. People come out of hypnosis whenever they please. The worst thing that can happen in hypnosis is that nothing happens.***

I then provide a definition of hypnosis to orient them to the reality of what they are about to experience and to create a positive expectation; which is a big part of the creation of change. What I tell clients is that hypnosis is a natural altered state of consciousness characterized by relaxation and a subconscious openness such that suggestions that are useful can be taken in deeply, owned, and acted upon. Feel free to alter this however you wish, particularly keeping in mind the subjects education and level of sophistication.

To begin the actual hypnosis, employ the following first induction strategy. As a prelude though, have the client sit comfortably in a chair, in a sustainable position, muscles relaxed, eyes closed. Assure them that there is nothing they need to do, that you will do all of the work, and that their unconscious will respond accordingly.

3

INDUCTION METHOD #1: DOUBLE BINDS

Now begin the double bind induction. Find a sample outline below. Be sure to use permissive language, that is; "you will" should be avoided in favor of "you may, or "you can". People generally don't like to be told what to do but rather prefer having their ability to choose validated and not challenged.

This double bind induction is also referred to as the "illusion of alternatives" because it offers a choice between two alternatives, both of which are desirable for the creation and experience of trance.

Say phrases like the following:

"You can go into hypnosis quickly or slowly."

"You may develop a light trance or a deep trance."

"You can allow yourself to drift into trance listening to the sound of my voice or to the sounds in the room."

"Perhaps you will begin to notice a lightness or maybe a comfortable heaviness as you flow down into hypnosis."

"You can move forward into trance by opening up to the creative possibilities inherent in hypnosis or you can focus on reconnecting with your own personal history of success."

After you are done saying these phrases slowly and with a deep voice, then you can repeat the phrases once or twice or better yet, make up more of your own. After that you can utilize other types of induction which you will find in the chapters that follow.

4

INDUCTION METHOD #2: CONSCIOUS – UNCONSCIOUS DISSOCIATIVE STATEMENTS

HEALTHY, NATURAL, AND PRODUCTIVE dissociation is a hallmark of being hypnotized. To foster dissociation in service of "creating trance" you can verbally separate the conscious and subconscious parts of the mind via the sentences below. Say them in order or randomly. Invent your own too. After you are done, you can repeat or go back to induction method #1 or onto the methods that follow! Do inductions until the subject is in hypnosis (more on how to tell that later). If the client is hypnotized then you can proceed to the intervention stage of trance work. If this induction is being used for self-hypnosis, it is best that it is audio taped as it is far too hard to think about what to say and still go into trance.

Conscious – Unconscious Dissociative Statements

Your Conscious Mind	Causal Link	Your Unconscious Mind
1. Is listening to my words	And	Is doing something else
2. May be interested in learning one thing	And	Is concerned with what's relevant
3. May have certain doubts	While	Understands and absorbs what you need
4. Is very linear	While	Can provide you with a mosaic of creative potentials
5. Intellectualizes, analyzes, and compartmentalizes	Just as	It is an infinite storehouse of talents, learnings and possibilities
6. May be easily diverted	Because	Can allow things to happen in your own best interest

It would be a good idea to sit down and make up your own conscious-subconscious dissociative statements and add them to these.

5

HYPNOTIC INDUCTION METHOD #3: ABC AND 1, 2, 3

This induction method consists of an age regression back in time to metaphorically teach the subject how to reconnect to past resources. By doing so, the client goes into trance as part of regressing. This induction accomplishes two things at once; entrancing the subject while also preparing them for the intervention phase of hypnosis by giving them an object lesson in resource retrieval (learning that they can learn to do something that appears horribly difficult at first). Implicit in the above statement is a very important point: *age regression should always be done to access historical moments of cognitive, emotional , and experiential strengths.* Regression back to traumatic experiences is a thorny hypnotic thicket that should be attempted by only the most advanced and credentialed hypnotists.

While the hypnotist can read the script below verbatim, feel free to be creative and riff off of it. Again, if after doing this and the client is not in trance, use methods #1 and #2 or method #4 which follows. Also, if this is to be used for autohypnosis (self hypnosis), it is best to record the induction. No matter if in person, on zoom, or a phone consult, you can record it on your device and send it to the subject electronically.

The induction below is a transcript of the actual work of the pioneering legendary hypnotist Milton Erickson M.D. His grammar, syntax, and usage has been preserved as spoken for accuracy of intent.

"And I'm going to talk about something that occurred in your childhood when you first went to school and had to learn to write the letters of the alphabet. It seemed like a terribly difficult task. All those letters, all those different shapes. Do you dot the "e, i" and cross the "i"? And where do you put the loop on the "b" and the "d" and the "p"? And how many bumps on the letter "m"? Gradually you formed a mental image of each letter, many mental images, because letters are in script and in print of various shapes and sizes and finally you had mental images located somewhere in your brain and you added mental images of persons and words and numbers and objects and even ideas. Not knowing at the time you were forming mental images.

While I've been talking to you your respiration has changed, your blood pressure has changed. Your muscle tone has changed and your muscle reflexes have changed. Close your eyes now and feel the sense of comfort. The more comfortable you feel the deeper into a trance you'll go.

In the trance state you can let your unconscious mind (pause) survey that vast array of learnings that you achieve, that you have achieved during your lifetime. There are many learnings that you've made without knowing it. Many of the learnings that were very important to you consciously have slipped into your unconscious mind and have become automatically useful to you and are used only at the right time, in the right situation.

Learning to walk was a very difficult task but you achieved it. Now you don't know just exactly how you walk down the street, how you move your feet and your legs, your arms, move your head, how far from the curb you slow down, what buildings you veer toward and what buildings you veer away from. You don't know which way you first move your head when you first reach an intersection. But you will look to the right and to the left and ahead. You'll make a lot of movements. You'll make a lot of movements even if there is no traffic of any kind.

When you first learned to drive a car that was a very big task to put on the brakes and stop at the intersection when you are traveling 10 miles an hour. But as you became an expert driver you could see a stop sign in the distance and it didn't make a bit of difference whether you were traveling 70, 60, 50, 40, 30 miles an hour. At the right time, at the right distance, with the right degree of force you applied the brake and rolled to a gentle stop. You don't even know how you measured that distance. You don't know what sense of body movement entered into it; what your peripheral vision told you and now I could sit in the back seat of the car you are driving and I would know at least a half a block in advance when you were going to turn right or left by your body language. I might know it even before you realize, "Oh, here's the street I turn on."

Your unconscious mind knows much more than you do. Your conscious mind has an awareness and it's oriented to the situation of the moment and so you're aware of desks and bookcases, wall hangings, telephone, which have nothing to do with your purpose in coming. But your unconscious mind can disregard all those irrelevant facts and pay attention to my words and pay attention to its own reactions."

Again, note the use of age regression for creating trance and then also to emphasize critical life lessons that will become current resources to be used for success in the present. Because of these dual happenings, this method winds up not only being a method of trance induction but a powerful change strategy as well.

6

INDUCTION METHOD #4: THE THREE-SENTENCE INDUCTION

This induction consists of three simple sentences that when verbalized puts a client into trance. It is easy to remember and replicate so there is never a need to tape, but of course you always can. As always, this induction can stand alone or be combined with the other three or even ones you have learned elsewhere. It was developed by G. Andrewartha.

In preparing for the Three-Sentence Induction, clients are given the following directions:

1. Explain to the subject you are going to use a very simple process of trance induction.
2. Have the subject sit comfortably with their feet resting on the floor, and their arms placed comfortably in their lap.
3. Commence the induction with sentence one.

Use a lower voice tone where indicated and develop a repetitive rhythm. The sentences are as follows:

1. You may allow (pause) what you are experiencing right now (pause) just to continue.
2. You may be really curious (pause) about just how comfortable (pause) you can be.
3. It's not necessary for you to (pause) go deeply into trance.

The first sentence effectively introduces the induction, gives permission, aids rapport, and matches the subject's experience. The subject needs only to continue doing whatever he or she is doing to be behaving appropriately.

The second sentence reinforces many of the elements of the first. The words "really curious" also introduce elements of drama and expectation, as well as age regression.

The third sentence utilizes potential resistance or noncompliance. It incorporates the embedded command "go deeply into trance." This also contains a double bind so a subject who chooses not to go deeply into trance may, implicitly, go lightly into trance.

By their nature and repetition, the sentences have proven to foster amnesia, time distortion, and dissociation. You will learn more about these three hypnotic phenomena in later chapters. Once trance is established, these sentences also deepen the trance experience.

The use of this technique can result in the induction of a moderate-to-deep trance in fifteen minutes or as rapidly as one minute.

7

INDUCTION METHOD #5: REGRESSION TO A PAST HIGHLY RELAXED STATE

IN ORDER FOR ANYTHING TO HAPPEN THAT YOU want to happen, in the chapters that are about to happen, you need to make deep relaxation happen. Relaxation is the foundation upon which you wish wishes and upon which they then come true. It is the fertile soil upon which you softly plant the seed of a hope. Then repeating this cycle over a few days provides the sunshine and water needed for the plant of intended new change to grow and flourish. More on this suggestive intentionality later but for now it is time to relax.

In the four prior inductions you learned indirect ways to engender relaxation. You did not suggest it directly, it was a byproduct of the induction at hand. Here you focus directly on creating relaxation, in either interpersonal hypnosis or self hypnosis.

Deep relaxation creates a state like and is as powerful as meditation, yoga, being in the zone, contemplative prayer and so on. It is a peak experience, can become a plateau experience, and tends to have a spiritual flavor.

Can't relax you say? SHUT UUUUUPPP! Everyone has a long history of at least intermittent *deep* relaxation. You claim you don't remember? Here, let me remind you of what you don't know that you know. Your subconscious is where your memories reside and all you need to do is tickle it to open up a treasure trove of vivid memories of relaxation. So, if one of the following releases a thread of a memory, pull on it gently. Go with it, make it vivid. Very vivid. Make it sensory. Very sensory. Sight, sounds, smells, tastes and touch blossom, in an ever more refined way.

Surely you can remember some of these……

- Laying on the beach
- Gently swinging in a hammock
- Gazing out at a magnificent vista such as the Grand Canyon or a mountain range
- Hiking on a trail in a forest.
- Listening to Gregorian chants
- When you first held your baby and went into a revery of gentle, soft gazing
- Daydreaming on a long easy car ride
- Sitting alone in one of the world's great cathedrals….
- A long relaxed jog
- Practicing your meditation and transcending

- Looking at beautiful art in an empty museum
- Feeling centered and gently focused immersed in a sweet and sublime yoga session
- Reflecting back on a hypnosis session you once had

These can all be developed and enriched with deep vivid sensory stimuli. One of the reasons for this is that cultivating immersion in all five sensory channels facilitates the experience of relaxation. It is no longer conceptual but sensory, and the mind responds accordingly. Another way of putting this is that anything the mind remembers vividly and in a sensory fashion becomes real once again.

Here are a couple of examples of how it might look. You would think to yourself (or say to another).......

"I am on the beach, just arrived. I lay down on a soft lounge chair with a thick terry cloth towel underneath me. I run one hand down the side of the towel immersing myself in the texture. My other hand goes into the sand and rolls the grains between my fingers. I am getting ever more relaxed. I focus so it is like this is the only thing that exists, the outside world with its stressors fades away. Waves lap. Saltwater air. Seagull soars and sounds. Kids play ball. Radio rock. Ice cream jingle man calls out. More and more relaxed."

Get the idea? Here is another.....

"Chartres, stained glass, colored glass, soar, saints,

saints, saints, candles, candles, candles, once mom said 'don't stare at candles in church, you will become hypnotized' but I want that. Relax. The deafening sound of silence. Old smells, incense smells, can kneel, don't kneel, old wood stroke with hand. Relax, relax, relax. One person walks, heels. Echo, echo, echo, click click, click, stop. Church bells, church bells, church bells, noon, hungry. Outside, the air is fresh. Souvenirs to buy. Lady old kerchief vail wrinkled face. Jambon, gruyere, baguette, Evian. Bus drives away. Chartres looms outstanding in its field. Smile and sigh"

Do this for whichever scenarios you choose, mine, yours, or theirs. Keep making it more and more vivid and you will build a solid foundation of relaxation. Upon that rock, you will build an attitudinal stance that is optimal for wishes to come to fruition. The specifics of how wishes can come to life is the topic of the next chapter.

8

RATIFICATION AND DEEPENING

AFTER INDUCTION, THE NEXT STEP IN HYPNOTIZING is ratification. Here is a succinct and efficient protocol for ratifying trance.

First though, let's define ratification. Ratification is the act of verbally stating or feeding back to the client that which you observe as indicative of trance. *Noticing indications of trance is how you know when to stop doing all those inductions!*

Beyond that, the purpose of ratification is to notify the client that he or she is cooperating by going into hypnosis. To this end you name the indicators or markers of hypnotic involvement that you observe. This serves an educational purpose in stating what they are doing correctly. In effect, you are telling them what to do more of so they can go deeper into hypnosis.

Another reason to ratify is to provide social reinforcement. By telling them what you see that is indicative of trance, you are telling them in effect that they are doing the right thing. This serves as a positive social reinforcement, as does the implication that they are pleasing you, the hypnotist.

A final reason to ratify is to train your eye to notice trance indicators. The more you observe, the more you know with regard to how well you are hypnotizing, and most importantly how well you are hypnotizing *this* particular client.

In summary, by ratifying you educate and train the client and yourself by providing observations and reinforcements with the end result that you hypnotize more effectively and the client gets hypnotized more efficiently.

Here is a list of things you might look for when ratifying:

- Very slow body movements
- Eventually, no body movement unless suggested (naturally occurring catalepsy)
- Ever deeper and slower breathing
- Pulse slows
- Muscles become very relaxed
- Head drooping
- Body tilting and becoming more asymmetrical
- Jaw slackening
- Upon awakening a greatly distorted sense of how much time has passed (ask)

- Upon reorienting reports having had feelings of dissociation
- Reports a quiet, silent mind

This is not an exhaustive list. Nonetheless, after your inductions, start feeding back to your client the things which you see them manifesting from the above list. As Milton Erickson would say, "observe, observe, observe".

Here is how ratification might sound:

"I can see you are going into hypnosis because your breath rate has slowed, your heart rate has slowed, and your muscles look very, very relaxed."

Or:

"I know that you're going down into trance because your head can't help itself from dropping down, your body is tilting off to one side and you probably don't even know it yet. Or if you do, you don't care. Also, your jaw is getting relaxed so your mouth is now open and you are even drooling a little bit. Don't worry about that, if it gets worse I will put a lobster bib on you (there will be no laughter, people lose their sense of humor in hypnosis, and you ratify that!).

Or:

The conversation upon awakening:

You: "How much time do you think passed?"

Subject: "Fifteen minutes, no, probably 10."

You: "It was actually 45 minutes...... you were deep in trance. This is proof that people can't tell time in hypnosis. And proof that you were deeply hypnotized ."

For reasons stated at the beginning of this chapter, most ratification should be done when the person is in trance. However, it tends to initially bring a person out of trance because the conscious mind gets focused and evaluative causing some beta wave brain activity and hence sympathetic nervous system arousal. Yet on the heels of that, the subconscious mind takes over and relaxes again and the person actually winds up going *deeper* into trance. So ratification is actually a method of deepening as well as helping one to attain the other hypnotic goals above.

In general, when a person goes in and out of hypnosis it deepens the trance. This is called "fractionation". It is one of the most powerful methods of deepening. You can effect this by ratifying or by simply bringing a person out of hypnosis repeatedly and then putting the person back in. It is a good alternative to doing more and more inductions.

You know you need to deepen if you do not see many signs of trance to ratify. So bring the person in and out of trance repeatedly…...fractionation.

Yet the simplest way to deepen, easier than using fractionation, is to do more inductions. Do as many as you need to until you see multiple signs of hypnosis taking place, such as when you can easily note them aloud to effect ratification.

To bring a person in and out of trance you would say something like this: "You can bring yourself a bit out of trance either going to a later stage of hypnosis or coming all the way out. If you come all the way out, you open your eyes and look at me and then immediately you'll go back down into an even deeper state of hypnosis that you have achieved previously here or anywhere else."

So that is how you ratify and deepen. Do it after your initial inductions. Have at it!

9

THE ART OF GIVING SUGGESTIONS - TO SELF AND OTHERS

Much attention has been given to self-hypnosis, both for adults and for children. When the topic of giving oneself suggestions in hypnosis is addressed, it is almost always as if it is simply a matter of saying words to oneself, once the induction has been completed. This approach limits the potential for effective self -suggestion because it frames the intervention as being linguistic and technical only. Having the proper mental stance or attitudinal position is, at least, as important as the words themselves.

It is vital to note though that while most of the chapters in this book are written for the person doing hypnosis to another, requiring a small mental gymnastics to make it work as self hypnosis, this chapter is written in the opposite way. So reverse the translation process for hetero-hypnosis. In the end, it does not matter much as what you say to another is what you would say to yourself in self hypnosis. And when you say something to another, they consciously endorse it and repeat it to their subconscious mind. All hypnosis is in effect self hypnosis.

I propose a set of illustrative metaphors that will enable the practitioner, child or adult, of self -hypnosis or interpersonal hypnosis to adopt an optimal psychological position vis-à-vis the suggestions being given such that they have maximum effect.

These metaphors harken to times in the past where an optimal mental attitude was present. As such, they provide a historical reference point and resource for the practitioner of self- hypnosis so that they can easily adopt a proper psychological position that will enable the desired suggestion to have a fantastic impact.

Please note that these illustrative metaphors are appropriate for all but the stodgiest adults. That is to say, no doubt there are some CPAs, engineers, and surgeons, who will balk at their playful and often regressive nature. Nonetheless, for most, they will serve as an ideal template with which to understand what is meant by an optimal mental attitude or stance.

Because most of these metaphors involve regression to childhood experiences, they also serve as an additional induction method, or deepening. As you will learn in the next chapter, eliciting any hypnotic phenomena, especially age regression, moves a person deeper into trance.

Self-suggestions are best conceived as personal wishes embedded in an optimal psychological framework. The wish alone is not enough. It must be put forth coming out of the right attitude that will enable the self to allow the wishes to be fulfilled.

The following metaphors will quickly serve to show subjects the correct way to wish their self-hypnotic wishes:

> "Everyone has had the experience of being presented with a birthday cake with candles on it. Your task then becomes to take a moment, close your eyes, get into a certain frame of mind, and make a wish for something to come true while seeking to blow out all the candles so that it does."

> "Many of us have seen a shooting star in the night sky. When we do, we quickly make a wish in the hopes that viewing this phenomenon will allow it to come true."

> "More commonly, all of us have seen the first star in the night sky. At that moment, we take the opportunity to offer up a wish that we hope will take place."

> "On Thanksgiving Day it is common for a dried out turkey wishbone to be grabbed at each end by two small children who then pull each end and break it. The one who gets the bigger piece either makes a wish on the spot, which he/she hopes to come true, or hopes that the wish that he made prior to the contest comes to fruition."

"Just about every one of us has had the opportunity to throw a coin into a fountain or a pool of water. Prior to tossing the coin you make a wish and then upon tossing the coin gently, hope that it will come true."

These metaphors are common everyday examples, many from childhood, that adeptly illustrate the optimal mental approach or attitude to giving oneself wishes or self-suggestions. We all secretly recognize that what we are hoping for is some shift in conscious or subconscious functioning, such that the environment reacts differently to us and our wish comes to fruition. It is the law of attraction.

I can not say it enough, so I will repeat myself. All hypnosis is in essence self- hypnosis, so the psychological positioning illustrated above can be utilized in interpersonal hypnosis. All hypnosis is self hypnosis because no matter what a hypnotist says, a client will repeat it to themselves, allowing it in, so long as the suggestion is palatable.

Please note that some of these metaphors may be culturally bound. Obviously if the metaphor is not found in a particular culture, it makes little sense to use it unless you are enchanting a person with possibilities that exist in other cultures.

When working in non-North American cultures, it can be interesting and useful to find out the contexts within which wishes are seen to actualize in that country. I can remember asking about this while teaching in Russia where there were many very interesting and unique examples of times when wishes might easily come to fruition. One that stands in mind concerns the notion that if a person is standing between two people of the same name it is lucky. Therefore, it is a superb time to make a wish for something you want to come true. That is to say if you have a man named Andre on your right and another man named Andre on your left, you have satisfied the conditions for good fortune with regard to any wish made.

This approach to making self-suggestion will increase the effectiveness of suggestions for change. Such has been my experience in over 30 years of clinical practice and I think it makes good clinical sense that hypnotic suggestions to oneself should be more than just a set of words introduced after an induction.

For those wishing to learn more about giving self-suggestions, read Dr. Richard Nongard's excellent book on the topic entitled "The Self Hypnosis Solution".

10

WHAT ARE HYPNOTIC PHENOMENA?

HYPNOTIC PHENOMENA ARE INCREDIBLY USEFUL IN resolving various issues. Here they are defined and described.

Hypnotic phenomena can be described as natural behavioral and experiential manifestations of the trance state. They include both subjectively experienced psychological events such as remembering, forgetting, distortions in one's sense of time, and alterations in perception, as well as observable events, such as the levitation of an arm or the automatic, unconsciously driven scribbling of words across a pad.

HERE ARE THE VARIETIES OF HYPNOTIC PHENOMENA:

Catalepsy is a special state of muscle tone and balance that permits the subject to sustain postures and positions for unusually long periods of time, without appreciable fatigue. It is accompanied by slowing down of all psychomotor activity and is the basis for other phenomena such as arm levitation.

AN ALTERATION IN ONE'S SENSE OF TIME IS ANOTHER hypnotic phenomenon that is commonly experienced by subjects even under conditions of light trance. Time becomes very subjective and dissociated from standard measures. A person in trance for 25 minutes, who thinks the trance has been only 10 minutes long, is experiencing **time contraction.** Someone who feels a 10-minute trance to be of half an hour in duration, experiences **time expansion.**

DISSOCIATION IS ONE OF THE MORE WIDELY recognized and experienced hypnotic phenomena. It is a separation of psychological states into conscious and unconscious, or a separation of emotions from thoughts, behaviors, and feelings. Dissociation may also be defined as "a mental process in which systems of ideas are split off from the normal personality and operate independently". Dissociation, apart from being a vehicle of intervention in its own right, is also the process by which the development of other hypnotic phenomena, such as age regression, automatic writing, pain control, and therapeutic hallucinations, take place. After all, it is the suspension of logical, rational, and intellectualized thoughts that allow these other, seemingly irrational or regressive, experiences to be brought forth into consciousness.

AMNESIA REFERS TO A FUNCTIONAL LOSS OF THE ability to recall or identify past experiences. It manifests, in its ability, to have subjects forget things that are generally considered impossible to forget, such as one's name and age. Amnesia can be induced in hypnosis either to ablate memories (of experience, affect, or cognition) that occurred prior to the trance or ablate those being created during the trance experience itself.

HYPERMNESIA REFERS TO AN ENHANCED MEMORY ability that transcends everyday recollection. This hypnotic phenomenon allows subjects to vividly remember memories in all their sensory detail.

THE PHENOMENON OF **AGE REGRESSION** IS PARTLY based upon the mechanisms of amnesia and hypermnesia. In the context of hypnosis, age regression allows one to re-experience memories of an earlier period. Age regressions differ from simple hypermnesia, in that, the subject *relives* rather than just remembers past events and, at times, experiences a return to the psychological state as it existed then. Thus, an adult can respond to suggestions to have amnesia for his or her adult years and return to the cognitive, affective, and behavioral experience of being a teenager. True age regressions like that, where there is a demonstrable suspension of adult faculties and motor responses, are more difficult to elicit than regressions where the subject retains adult faculties and behaviors, and simply re-experiences an earlier time/memory.

Future progression (also referred to as **age progression, future orientation** and **pseudo-orientation** in time) is the hypnotic phenomenon that disorients the subject away from the present and into the future. The experience can be one of seeing the future self, talking to the future self, or being the future self, with access to the imagined thoughts and feelings of the older self.

Negative and positive hallucinations refer to alterations in the subject's experience of sensory stimuli. Hallucinations can involve any of the sensory systems of vision, hearing, taste, touch, and smell. Negative hallucinations refer to the person *not* perceiving a stimulus that actually does exist in the immediate environment. For instance, a person who is sensitive to cigarette odor and who works in an environment where smoking is present may be helped to reduce her perception of cigarette smoke in the air via negative olfactory hallucinations. A teenager taunted at school can learn to effect negative auditory hallucinations for the comments of his pesky or cruel peers. A sales manager anxious about giving an oral report to a roomful of supervisors can use negative visual hallucinations to blur the clarity with which she recognizes their faces.

Hypnotic blindness, color blindness, and deafness (extremes of the phenomenon of negative hallucination) are very achievable. This ability of the body to ignore the perception of specific sensory stimuli is one of the bases for using anesthesia and analgesia for pain control.

Positive hallucinations refer to a person's experience of a sensory stimulus that is not actually present. Thus, a person can use the positive olfactory hallucination of liniment as a post-hypnotic cue to gear up for an athletic competition. Positive auditory hallucinations can help a self-doubting, novice therapist recall the encouraging words of a respected supervisor or the positive feedback from a satisfied client. That same sales manager, anxious about her oral report can, alternately, be helped to create a positive visual hallucination vis-à-vis her audience of supervisors, wherein she experiences the room filled instead with family and friends or even strangers.

. . .

AUTOMATIC WRITING IS A HYPNOTIC PHENOMENON that is an outgrowth of a dissociation between conscious and unconscious mental functioning. The subject, in response to direct or indirect suggestions to write, does in fact write with pen and paper but without conscious awareness, vigilance, or interference. The material may include previously repressed ideas or memories useful in propelling the client toward health. It may give rise to associations that the client then applies toward the problem resolution, or it may provide a new perspective on the problem or a solution. Also, the process of uncensored writing may actually turn out to be the most important aspect of the experience, allowing for re-engagement with a more liberated, creative, and disinhibited part of the self. **Automatic drawing** or **painting** would be, of course, the artistic correlates to automatic writing.

POSTHYPNOTIC SUGGESTION REFERS TO THE execution, at some later (post-trance) time or date, of instructions or suggestions given during trance. A couple using hypnosis for childbirth can be told together in trance that their first sighting of the hospital when they drive up during labor will automatically begin the upper/lower body dissociation and anesthesia sensations practiced previously in session.

. . .

ANALGESIA REFERS TO A DULLING IN ONE'S awareness of pain whereas **anesthesia** refers to a complete lack of awareness of pain. These hypnotic phenomena are especially useful in pain control cases where medication is contraindicated (i.e., risk of allergic reaction, or a history of drug addiction and/or abuse) or is unavailable. Pain is often a part of many sexual problems.

HYPERESTHESIA IS AN ENHANCED SENSITIVITY TO physical sensations such as touch, warmth, or coolness. Pain is not a fixed response to a painful stimulus but rather a sensation, the perception of which is modified by past experiences, expectation, and cultural attitudes. This idea provides the essential underpinnings for the viability and applicability of pain control measures such as analgesia, anesthesia, and hyperesthesia.

HYPNOTIC DREAMING ENTAILS THE SUBJECT'S capacity to have, either in session or at home during sleep, a directed therapeutic dream that is an immediate by-product of the suggestion given during the session.

IDEOMOTOR MOVEMENT INVOLVES THE BODY'S motor system reacting and acting as if directed by the unconscious mind, with the result that the person feels the movement to be avolitional, that is, that the conscious mind is a passive observer. **Arm levitation** is one example of ideomotor movement.

HYPNOTIC PHENOMENA ARE VERY HELPFUL IN resolving problems. The following chapter describes how to elicit and produce hypnotic phenomena in trance work.

11

DOING IT: HYPNOTIC PHENOMENA

At this point it's important that I elucidate a specific protocol through which hypnotic phenomena can be elicited. The phenomena protocol is as follows:

1. Seeding
2. Language-based suggestions for the phenomena
    —— a. Presuppositions
    —— b. Direct suggestion
    —— c. Double binds
    —— d. Conscious/subconscious dissociated statements
3. Metaphors
4. Natural examples from everyday life
5. Symbols
6. Follow-through

1. SEEDING

The first thing a person using hypnosis to elicit hypnotic phenomena can do is **_seed_** the hypnotic phenomena. Seeding is the hypnotic equivalent of the literary device of foreshadowing. In seeding, you hint at what is to come in the hypnosis proper. Seed prior to the actual hypnotic session and the hypnotic intervention as a way of "priming the pump".

Examples of this method are as follows:

> "Become very curious about what kind of delightfully disarming experience you'll have in trance today." (Arm levitation)

> "As you settle into a comfortable trance depth, your unconscious mind can begin to draw its own conclusions about the matter at hand." (Automatic drawing)

> "Wasn't it easy for you to have lost awareness of the traffic sounds outside? Go ahead and override the needs of your conscious mind to be aware of everything and let your unconscious teach you about the beauty and simplicity of absence." (Negative hallucination)

2. LANGUAGE-BASED SUGGESTIONS

In the hypnotic work proper there are four major language-based ways of eliciting hypnotic phenomena. First, the therapist can use ***presuppositions***. Presuppositions constitute therapeutic assumptions. Here you assume that something is going to happen and therefore the subject believes accordingly. It is an indirect way of getting the client to believe that something is true. They begin expecting what they might experience, and in doing so they begin to create it.

Examples of this method are as follows:

"Your first inkling that a dream is about to take place can be your cue to go ever more deeply into trance." (Hypnotic dreaming)

"Once you recognize your perception of time/space/sensation beginning to alter, your unconscious self can begin to speculate about how best to apply that different and special experience of the world." (Time distortion with dissociation and positive and negative hallucination)

"When you first wonder whether it is warmth or numbness you feel in your hands, you can smile with pride at how well your body responds to hypnosis." (Catalepsy)

A SECOND LANGUAGE-BASED WAY OF NOTICING hypnotic phenomena is ***direct suggestion***. This is the easiest and most obvious method of eliciting hypnotic phenomena, in that you simply and forthrightly suggest it.

Examples of this method are as follows:

"Invite that whimsical part of you to lift your hand — let it enchant you!" (Arm levitation)

"Slowly, ever so slowly, slow down inside and let time follow." (Time distortion)

"You, too, can be this imaginary great erotic lover right here, as a grown-up, whether or not you had one or more imaginary friends as a child. Why not ask your unconscious mind to open up those memory stores and show you again how easy it is to drum up whomever you need." (Positive visual and auditory hallucinations)

DOUBLE BINDS CONSTITUTE A THIRD LANGUAGE-based way in which hypnotic phenomena can be elicited. With double binds you offer an illusion of alternatives. After you have offered such, the client feels a freedom to choose from what you've presented; two possibilities, either of which moves the client in the desired direction.

Examples of this method are as follows:

> "Perhaps it will be your left hand that begins to feel light and rise up or maybe it will be your right hand that will feel an increased sense of levity." (Arm Levitation)

> "You can develop a deep, profound, and robust amnesia for any bad putt that rattles you immediately after you make that putt, or you can develop that immense and unreachable amnesia the minute you go to make your next putt." (Amnesia)

Conscious/subconscious dissociative statements are the fourth and final language-based way in which hypnotic phenomena can be elicited. With these suggestions the client's conscious mind is coaxed to do one productive thing related to a hypnotic phenomenon while her subconscious mind is simultaneously coaxed into doing something complementary, yet different.

. . .

Examples of this method are as follows:

> "Your conscious mind can let go of certain fragments of thoughts while your unconscious mind lets go of entire texts of ideas." (Amnesia)

> "Your conscious mind can become aware of feeling wistful while your unconscious mind tenderly reveals old thoughts that have some bearing on the things we spoke about today." (Hypermnesia)

3. METAPHORS

Metaphors are often very helpful in eliciting hypnotic phenomena. A metaphor in our context is a story or anecdote that contains, within it, suggestions for the development of the hypnotic phenomenon in question.

Examples of sample metaphors designed to induce a specific hypnotic phenomena are as follows:

- Fog lifting, re-assembly of jigsaw puzzles, a series of knots being untied one by one. (Hypermnesia)
- Circuit breaker, dials, "thick skin". (Anesthesia/analgesia)
- Clocks with worn-out batteries, cuckoo clocks with worn-out mechanisms, daylight

savings time, running through water. (Time expansion or elongation)

4. NATURAL EXAMPLES

Natural examples of a hypnosis-like or pseudo-hypnotic nature drawn from everyday life constitute still yet another wonderful way of eliciting hypnotic phenomena. They illustrate the hypnosis that occurs in ordinary life and as such they can show people that the hypnotic phenomena we're seeking to create are not very unusual, but are in fact sometimes part and parcel of our day. While using natural examples, subjects get the sense that they are not producing something alien but instead something familiar.

EXAMPLES OF NATURAL HYPNOSIS-LIKE SITUATIONS that can elicit hypnotic phenomena are as follows:

- Szechuan chicken, hot salsa, new shoes, professional perfume developers. (Hyperesthesia)
- Physiological habituation to sound/temperature, absorption in a movie to the exclusion of hearing the telephone ring. (Negative hallucination)
- The childhood game of red light/green light, Simon Says, sprinters at the block, divers poised at the 10-meter board. (Catalepsy)

5. SYMBOLS

Therapists can use symbols to elicit hypnotic phenomena. When you use a symbol, you are using a living representation of the hypnotic phenomenon in question.

Examples of symbols that can be developed in hypnosis to elicit a hypnotic phenomenon are as follows:

- Mannequin (Arm levitation and catalepsy)
- Elephant toy (Hypermnesia)
- Etch-A-Sketch (Automatic drawing)
- Polygraph (Automatic writing)
- Nursery rhyme (Age regression)

6. FOLLOW-THROUGH

After making these suggestions designed to produce hypnotic phenomena, it's useful to follow through. Following through is as important in hypnosis as it is in athletics or sales. Therefore, after the hypnosis proper is over it is useful to mention things that will help to consolidate the intervention that was promoted during the session.

Examples of this method are as follows:

- Repeat what was said during the hypnosis.
- Say it in a different way.
- Give post-hypnotic suggestions to enable the effects to be re-experienced later.
- Make verbal and visual bridges between what occurred in hypnosis and everyday life.
- Ask the client how she thinks she might use in everyday life the intervention just suggested in the hypnotic session.

Sometime after eliciting the hypnotic phenomena for intervention, but before ending trance following through, be sure to connect what you have produced to the problem at hand. In other words, after you have elicited catalepsy for example, attach that solution to the client's issue. For example here is what you might say in the latter moments of trance work with someone who suffers premature ejaculation. "Now that your arm is erect, rigid, still, and a bit numb, you are welcome to intermittently, as needed, experience this when you have sex and you won't come early, you will last." That connection seals the deal!

For more information on hypnotic phenomena and how to produce it, read my book "The Handbook of Hypnotic Phenomena in Psychotherapy" (by Dr. John H. Edgette). And yes, that is a direct suggestion!

12

DE-HYPNOTIZING YOUR CLIENT

Bringing your client out of hypnosis is ridiculously easy. Simply tell them to come out of hypnosis. Yup, that is right! Examples of exactly what to say are at the end of this chapter.

While anyone can be hypnotized, if they want to be, no one can be hypnotized if they don't want to be. What this means is that no one is "**UNDER YOUR CONTROL**", or mine, thank goodness. I sure don't want that responsibility! What that also means is that anyone can come out of hypnosis if they wish to. Moreover, research has shown that if no suggestions are given for ending the trance then almost everyone automatically comes out on their own in minutes. So even if you remain silent or even leave the room, things will work out just fine! Anyone that does not come out of hypnosis is making an indirect communication about the experience of being in trance.

So a client choosing not to de-hypnotize may be

commenting on the issue that they came to session with ("I'm stuck") OR they may be making a statement about the relationship with you ("I expected having more time with you") OR they may be super suggestible and responding to your very words ("You can come out of hypnosis at a pace that is right for you").

No matter the reason, a sure fire way to bring a person out of the trance is to simply tell them you are going to touch them on the hand only and then wiggle their hand. This should be left for last. First, reiterate over and over until the person comes out of trance, the ordinary de-hypnotizing suggestions which you will see below.

Here are some examples of typical and everyday ways of bringing a person out of hypnosis:

> "You can allow yourself to begin coming out of trance, you can begin cracking your eyes and moving your hands, then opening your eyes wider and moving your arms and moving your legs a little bit, and then you can rise up and wake up all over."

> "You can begin to come up at a very fine pace, perhaps the same way that you get out of bed in the morning when you don't need to hit the snooze alarm, but you don't just jump out. You stretch, open your eyes, and then sit up."

> "You can begin to come out of trance, but do know that when I say come out of trance, what I mean is

that you'll be more social, you'll be more physically active, your conscious mind will be more active, and you'll be more interactive. While all of that happens, you can keep and hold onto all of the good feelings that you have inside, all the relaxation, all the peace of mind, all the feelings of centeredness. Coming out of trance means that you can keep these things in an ongoing way while being more physically, consciously, and socially active."

If a person does not come out of hypnosis right away you can, as I said earlier, repeat the de-hypnotizing instructions a number of times and then tell them you're going to touch their hand and move it and wiggle it while still continuing to suggest that they exit the hypnotic, altered state. Just the same, if you wish to individualize the trance ending instructions, taking into consideration what you deem to be issues you think are central to the situation at hand, then you can say something like what is contained in the two examples below:

"Perhaps you want more time to work with me, and that's why you are remaining in trance. If that is in fact the case, just know that when you come out of hypnosis ***now*** we will be making appointments for the future and you're welcome to make as many as you would find useful."

"You want to stay hypnotized. That is just fine. Stay hypnotized for as long as you'd like, 15 minutes or half an hour, even a couple of hours or more. I'm going to see my next patient in the other office so when you do decide to come out of hypnosis simply leave through the waiting room, as you always do."

Now you know how to bring a person out of trance, and in fact know all the stages of hypnosis practice doing full inductions with volunteers or clients that you are seeing pro bono. More on this in the next chapter.

13

ENDING THIS TRANCE

THE TITLE OF THIS CHAPTER SPEAKS TO THE FACT that as you read about hypnosis you go into hypnosis. Why would this be? It happens because as you read you experienced the words going into your subconscious mind and influencing it. Also, you probably imagined what it all would feel like in self hypnosis. Anything imagined vividly to some significant extent becomes reality! And NOW is the time to come out of trance and reorient toward the external world.

What this portion of the external world is up to is wrapping up this book. You have read and hopefully practiced the various stages of trance. Prep, Induction, ratification, deepening, giving verbal suggestions, using hypnotic phenomena, and trance termination.

So now is the time to live it. Learn stage hypnosis. Learn how to give suggestions for habit change. Teach people self hypnosis for relaxation and personal change.

Be the life of the party! BUT MOST OF ALL HAVE FUN!

14

LIST OF HYPNOTIC STEPS

- Prep of Client
- Induction (One or More)
- Ratification
- Deepening
- Giving of Suggestions
- Use of Multiple Types of Hypnotic Phenomena
- De-Hypnotizing of Client
- Discussion of Experience-Useful and Not Useful Aspects

ABOUT DR. JOHN H. EDGETTE

Dr. John H. Edgette received his doctoral degree in clinical psychology in 1985 from Hahnemann Medical College and Graduate School in Philadelphia, PA. He had practiced as a psychotherapist for over 30 years in agencies, clinics, group practices, and private practice.

Now practicing as a sexologist, life coach, and certified hypnosis consultant, he was licensed as a clinical psychologist in Iowa, Illinois, and Pennsylvania. He is the author of 3 books and over 7 journal articles. His works have been translated into 7 languages. He has been asked to give keynote addresses and seminars at over 50 professional conferences and has taught in over 30 states and 15 countries around the world.

Dr. John Edgette is available to practitioners via Zoom or FaceTime for individual consultations and advice regarding clients. Also, questions about hypnosis are welcome. He is also available for sessions with any individual having problems of any kind.

For more information call, text, e-mail, or FaceTime him at:
Phone: 1 917 806 1850
Text: 1 917 806 1850
E Mail: john@edgettetherapy.com

Visit Dr. John H. Edgette online at
www.edgettetherapy.com

ALSO BY DR. JOHN H EDGETTE

Get Your Kink On: Dos and Don'ts of Sexual Exploration

Hypnotic Erotic: A Practitioners Guide to Sexual Healing (Sexuality Series)

Psych Horse Handicapping: Using Your Head to Win by a Head and Be Ahead

Handbook Of Hypnotic Phenomena In Psychotherapy

Winning the Mind Game: Using Hypnosis in Sport Psychology

www.ingramcontent.com/pod-product-compliance
Lightning Source LLC
Chambersburg PA
CBHW071914070526
44583CB00016B/1993